EASY PIANO

MY FIRST GERSHWIN SONG BOOK

A TREASURY OF FAVORITE SONGS TO PLAY

Photos courtesy of Photofest

GERSHWIN® and GEORGE GERSHWIN® are registered trademarks of Gershwin Enterprises
IRA GERSHWIN™ is a trademark of Gershwin Enterprises
PORGY AND BESS® is a registered trademark of Porgy And Bess Enterprises

ISBN 978-1-4950-6291-9

HAL•LEONARD®
CORPORATION
7777 W. BLUEMOUND RD. P.O. BOX 13819 MILWAUKEE, WI 53213

In Australia Contact:
Hal Leonard Australia Pty. Ltd.
4 Lentara Court
Cheltenham, Victoria, 3192 Australia
Email: ausadmin@halleonard.com.au

Visit Hal Leonard Online at
www.halleonard.com

THE GERSHWIN BROTHERS

Icons of American song, George and Ira Gershwin will never be forgotten. The famous song-writing team of brothers wrote dozens of scores for Broadway and Hollywood musicals, including many individual hit songs that have helped define the Great American Songbook. Their music has been hailed as the first truly "American" popular song. The incredible artistry of their work is seen in the brilliant marriage of George's distinctively jazz-influenced harmonies and rhythms with Ira's witty lyrics and creative wordplay.

Both brothers were born in Brooklyn, New York, to Russian immigrants. Ira, born in 1896, started his professional life working as a cashier in his father's business while attending College of the City in New York. George, born two years later in 1898, left school at age 15 to work as a "song-plugger" on Tin Pan Alley. Within three years he had published several songs. His first big hit was "Swanee" with lyrics by Irving Caesar in 1919. George also found success as a pianist and conductor. His orchestral classics "Rhapsody in Blue," "An American in Paris," and "Concerto in F" continue to be programmed by major orchestras worldwide.

The Gershwin's first collaboration was the song "The Real American Folk Song (Is a Rag)" heard in the show LADIES FIRST. Because he was sensitive to George's early success, Ira used the pen name Arthur Francis. As Arthur Francis, Ira's first Broadway collaboration was with Vincent Youmans in the show TWO LITTLE GIRLS IN BLUE in 1921. When George and Ira teamed up in 1924 Ira dropped the pen name. Their first joint Broadway hit was the musical LADY, BE GOOD! They worked exclusively with each other from 1924 until George's untimely death in 1937.

After George's death, Ira stopped writing for almost three years before continuing to write lyrics, working with collaborators Harold Arlen, Jerome Kern, Kurt Weill and others. He published the autobiographical *Lyrics on Several Occasions* in 1959, a unique, annotated collection of his lyrics. In addition, Ira annotated all of the Gershwin manuscripts and materials consigned to the Library of Congress. He died at his home in Beverly Hills in 1983, at the age of 86.

An American in Paris

By GEORGE GERSHWIN

To Coda ⊕

a little slower

poco rit.

Allegretto

D.S. al Coda

CODA

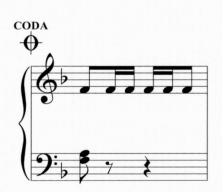

Bidin' My Time

Music and Lyrics by GEORGE GERSHWIN
and IRA GERSHWIN

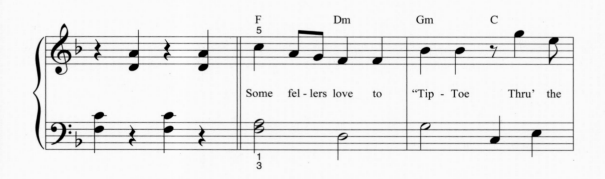

Some fel - lers love to "Tip - Toe Thru' the

Tu - lips;" some fel - lers go on

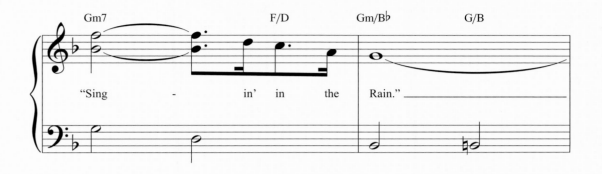

"Sing - in' in the Rain." _____

_____ Some fel - lers keep on "Paint - in' Skies with

Sun - shine." _____ Some fel - lers must go

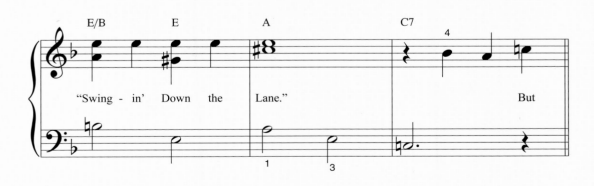

"Swing - in' Down the Lane." But

EMBRACEABLE YOU

EMBRACEABLE YOU

Music and Lyrics by GEORGE GERSHWIN
and IRA GERSHWIN

arms   a - bout   you.   Don't   be   a

naugh – ty   ba – by,   Come to   pa – pa, come to   pa – pa, do!

My   sweet   em – brace – – a – ble   you!

you!

BUT NOT FOR ME

Music and Lyrics by GEORGE GERSHWIN
and IRA GERSHWIN

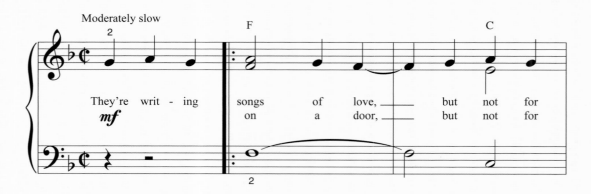

They're writ-ing songs of love,___ but not for
on a door,___ but not for

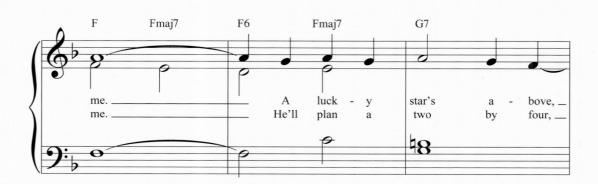

me.___ A luck-y star's a-bove,___
me.___ He'll plan a two by four,___

___ but not for me.
___ but not for me.
With love to lead the way ___
I know that love's a game; ___

- so, luck - y day!
- ler needs a friend.

Al - though I
When ev - 'ry

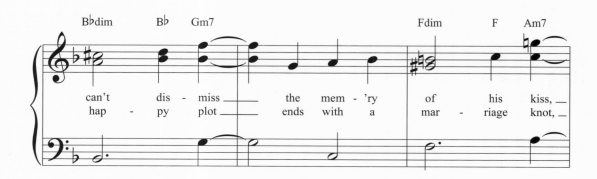

can't dis - miss the mem - 'ry of his kiss,
hap - py plot ends with a mar - riage knot,

I guess he's not for
and there's no knot for

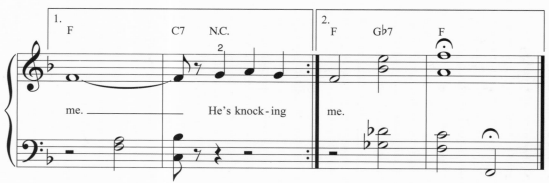

me.
He's knock - ing me.

A Foggy Day
(In London Town)

Music and Lyrics by GEORGE GERSHWIN
and IRA GERSHWIN

Freely, with motion

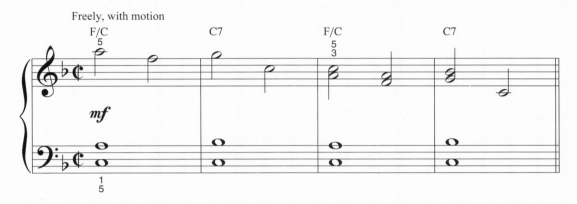

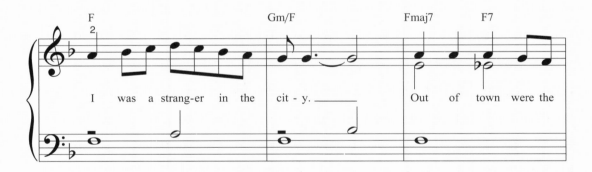

I was a strang-er in the cit-y. ___ Out of town were the

peo-ple I knew. I had a feel-ing of self-pit-y, ___ what to

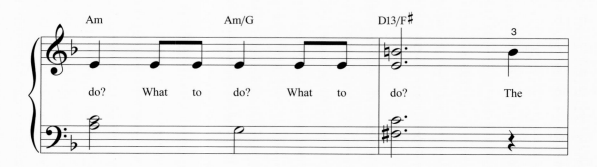

do? What to do? What to do? The

out - look was de - cid - ed - ly blue. _____ But as I

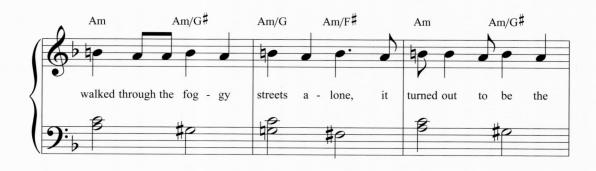

walked through the fog - gy streets a - lone, it turned out to be the

luck - iest day I've known. _____ A

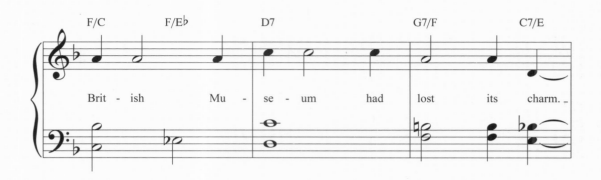

F/C   F/E♭   D7   G7/F   C7/E

Brit - ish Mu - se - um had lost its charm.

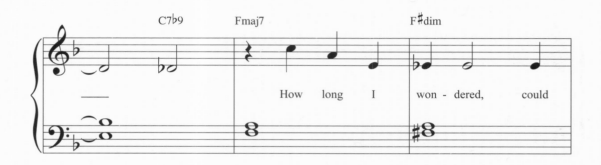

C7♭9   Fmaj7   F♯dim

How long I won - dered, could

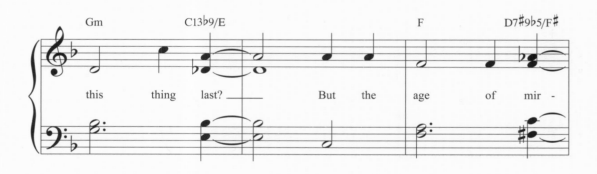

Gm   C13♭9/E   F   D7♯9♭5/F♯

this thing last? But the age of mir -

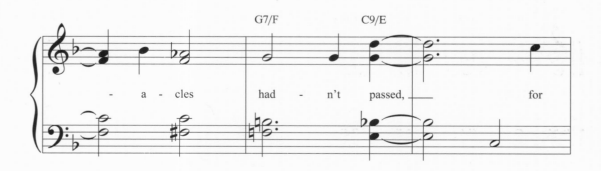

G7/F   C9/E

- a - cles had - n't passed, for

FASCINATING RHYTHM

Music and Lyrics by GEORGE GERSHWIN
and IRA GERSHWIN

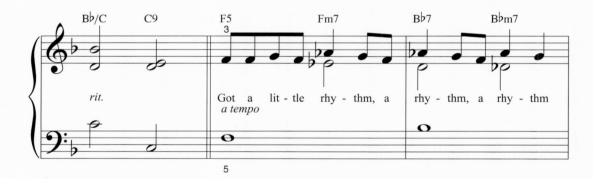

Got a lit-tle rhy-thm, a rhy-thm, a rhy-thm

that pit-a-pats through my brain. brain.

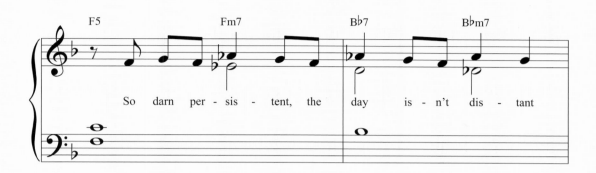

So darn per - sis - tent, the   day   is - n't   dis - tant

when it - 'll   drive   me   in - sane.

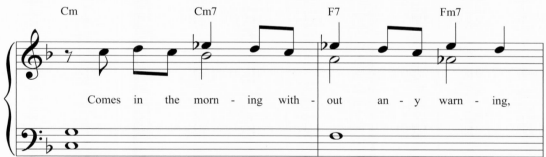

Comes   in   the   morn - ing   with - out   an - y   warn - ing,

and   hangs   a - round ___   all   day.

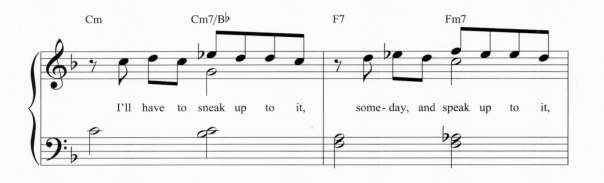

I'll have to sneak up to it, some-day, and speak up to it,

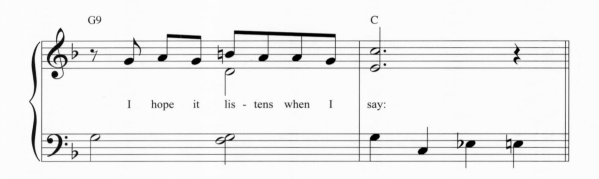

I hope it lis - tens when I say:

Fas - ci - nat - ing rhy - thm you've got me on the go! Fas - ci -

nat - ing rhy - thm, I'm all a - quiv - er.

What a mess you're mak-ing! The neigh-bors want to know why I'm

al-ways shak-ing just like a fliv-er. Each morn-ing

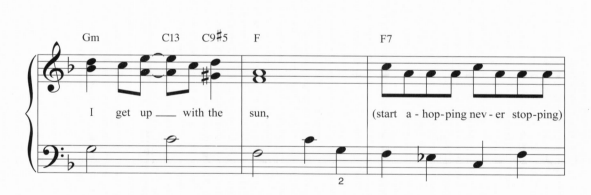

I get up ___ with the sun, (start a-hop-ping nev-er stop-ping)

to find at night, no work ___ has been done.

I know that once it did – n't mat – ter but

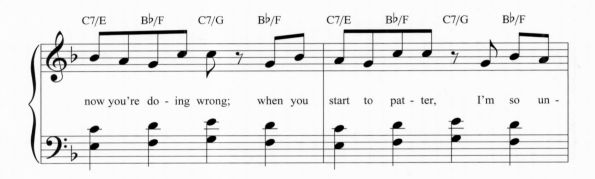

now you're do – ing wrong; when you start to pat – ter, I'm so un –

hap – py. Won't you take a day off? De –

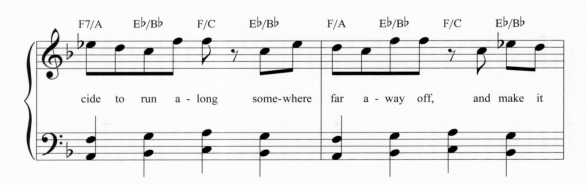

cide to run a – long some-where far a – way off, and make it

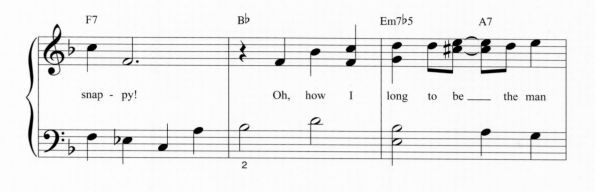

snap - py!　　　Oh, how I long to be ___ the man

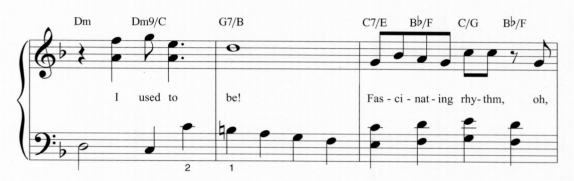

I used to be!　　　Fas - ci - nat - ing rhy - thm,　oh,

won't you stop pick - ing on　me!

me!

I Got Plenty O' Nuttin'

I Got Plenty O' Nuttin'

Music and Lyrics by GEORGE GERSHWIN,
DuBOSE and DOROTHY HEYWARD and IRA GERSHWIN

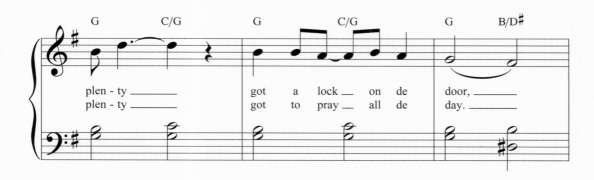

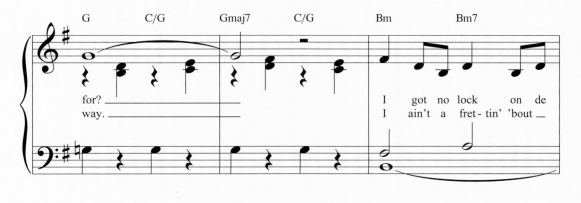

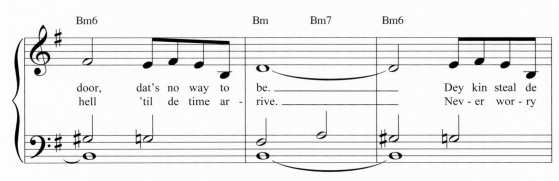

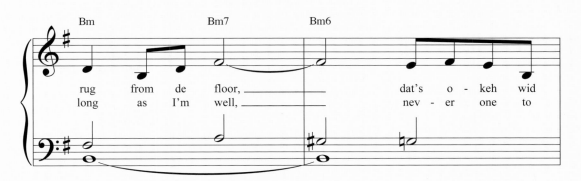

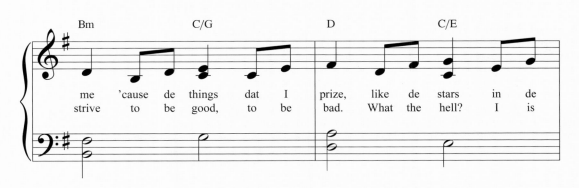

skies, all are free. _____ }
glad I's a-live. _____ }
Oh, I got plen-ty o'

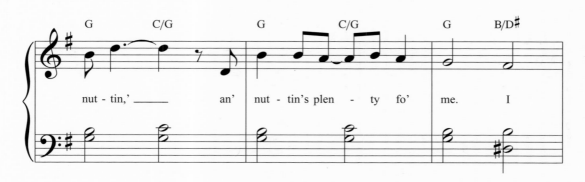

nut-tin,' _____ an' nut-tin's plen — ty fo' me. I

got my gal, got my song, got heb-ben the whole day

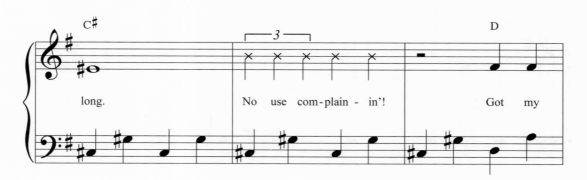

long. No use com-plain-in'! Got my

I Loves You, Porgy

Music and Lyrics by GEORGE GERSHWIN,
DuBOSE and DOROTHY HEYWARD and IRA GERSHWIN

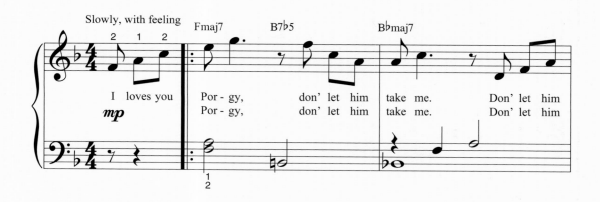

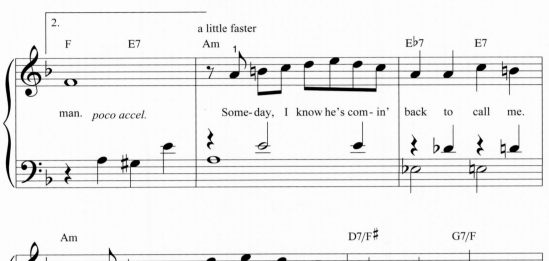

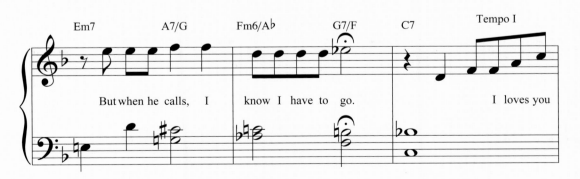

Por- gy, don' let him take me. Don' let him han-dle me an' drive me

mad. If you kin keep me, I wants to stay here wid you for-

ev - er, I got my man, wid you for-

ev - er, _____ I got my man. _____

SUMMERTIME

Music and Lyrics by GEORGE GERSHWIN,
DuBOSE and DOROTHY HEYWARD
and IRA GERSHWIN

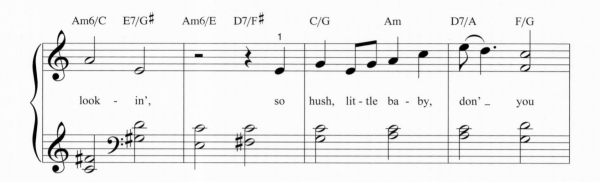

look - in', so hush, lit - tle ba - by, don' _ you

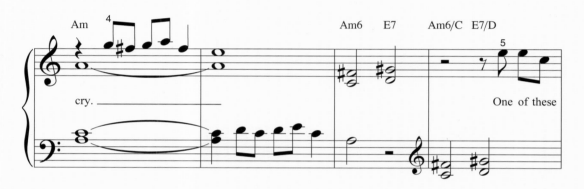

cry. _____ One of these

morn - in's you goin' to rise __ up sing - in', then you'll

spread yo' wings an' you'll take __ the sky. _____

I GOT RHYTHM

I GOT RHYTHM

Music and Lyrics by GEORGE GERSHWIN
and IRA GERSHWIN

Moderately, somewhat rubato

Days can be

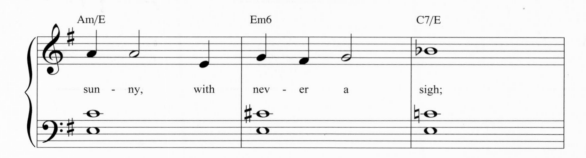

sun - ny,   with   nev - er a   sigh;

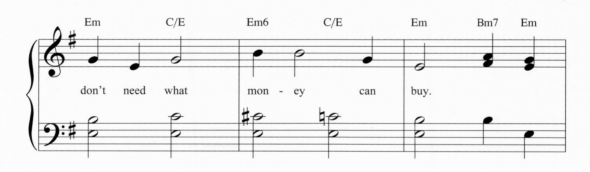

don't need what   mon - ey   can   buy.

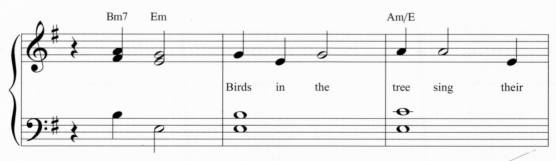

Birds   in   the   tree sing their

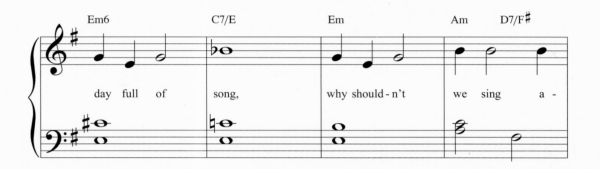

day full of   song,   why should-n't   we sing a -

long?   I'm   chip - per

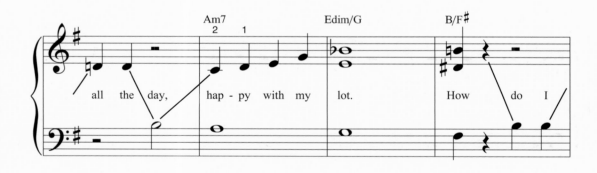

all the day,   hap - py with my   lot.   How   do I

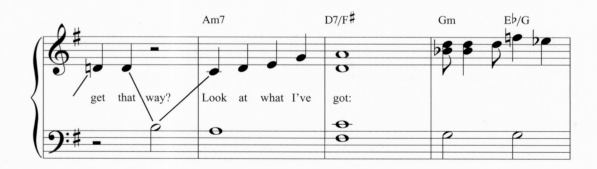

get that way?   Look at what I've   got:

pas - tures; ___ I ___ got my man. ___ Who could

ask for an - y - thing more? Old ___ Man

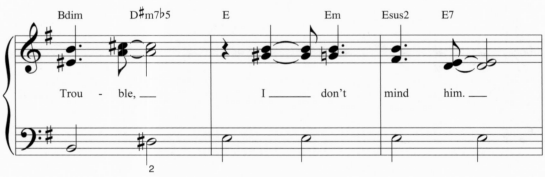

Trou - ble, ___ I ___ don't mind him. ___

You ___ won't find him ___ 'round ___ my

For You, For Me, For Evermore

Music and Lyrics by GEORGE GERSHWIN
and IRA GERSHWIN

Par - a - dise can - not re -
fuse us, nev - er such a hap - py pair!
Ev - 'ry - bod - y must ex - cuse us if we walk on
air.
All the shad - ows now will lose us,

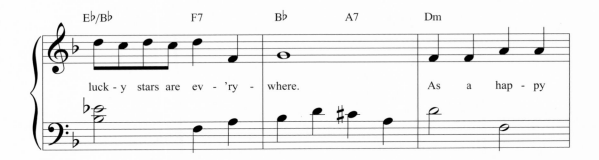

luck - y stars are ev - 'ry - where.   As   a   hap - py

be - ing,   here's what   I'm   fore - see - ing: For

poco rit.

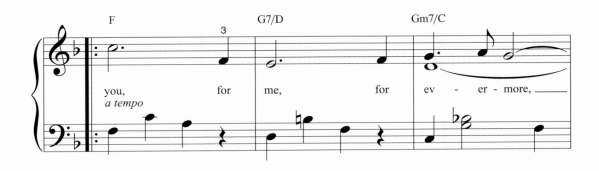

you,   for   me,   for   ev - er - more, ____

a tempo

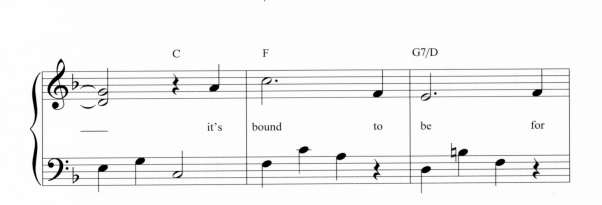

____   it's   bound   to   be   for

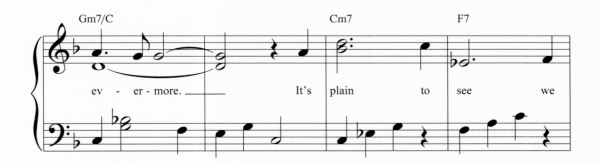

ev - er - more. ___ It's plain to see we

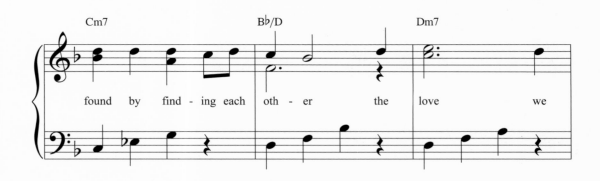

found by find - ing each oth - er the love we

wait - ed for. ____ *rit.* I'm yours, *a tempo* you're

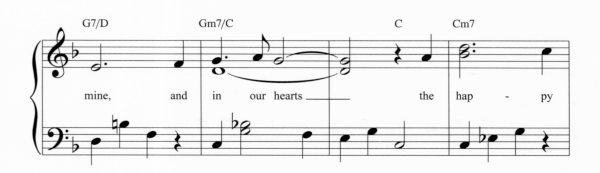

mine, and in our hearts ___ the hap - py

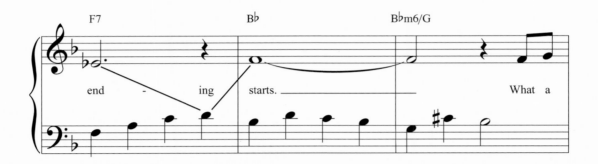

end - ing starts. _____ What a

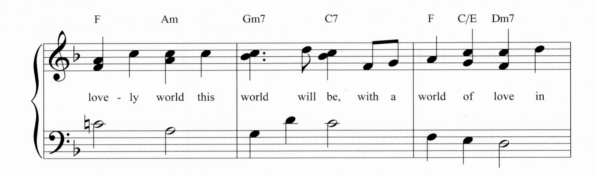

love - ly world this world will be, with a world of love in

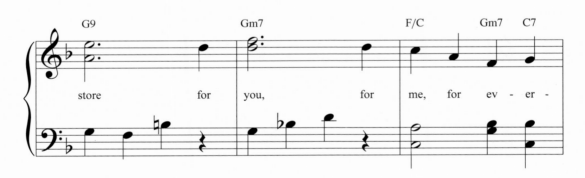

store for you, for me, for ev - er -

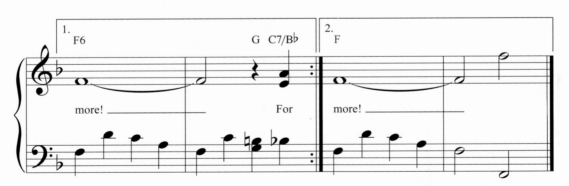

more! _____ For more! _____

FUNNY FACE

Music and Lyrics by GEORGE GERSHWIN
and IRA GERSHWIN

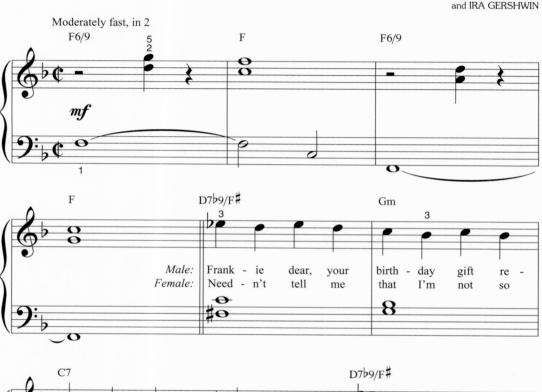

Moderately fast, in 2

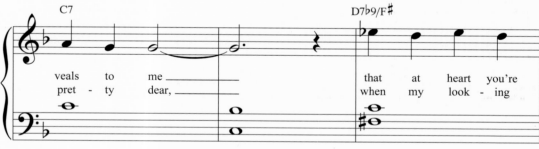

Male: Frank-ie dear, your birth-day gift re-
Female: Need-n't tell me that I'm not so

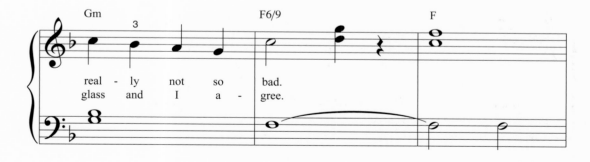

veals to me _____ that at heart you're
pret-ty dear, _____ when my look-ing

real-ly not so bad.
glass and I a-gree.

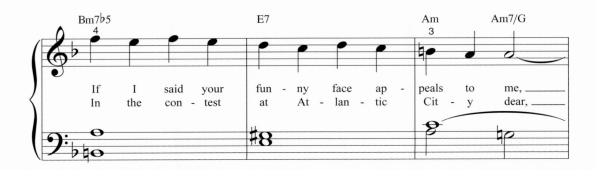

If   I   said   your   fun - ny   face   ap -   peals   to   me,
In   the   con - test   at   At - lan - tic   Cit - y   dear,

please don't think I've   sud - den - ly   gone
Miss   A - mer - i - ca   I'd   nev - er

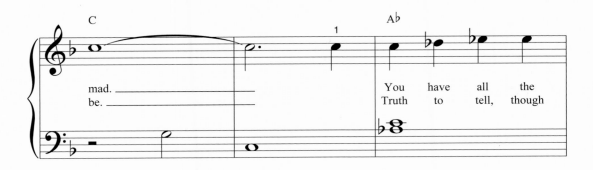

mad.   You   have   all   the
be.   Truth   to   tell,   though

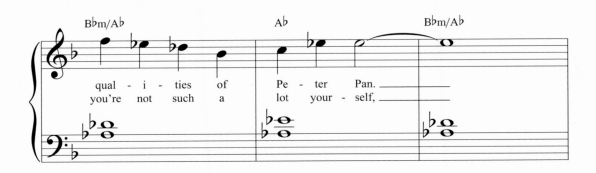

qual - i - ties   of   Pe - ter   Pan.
you're not such   a   lot   your - self,

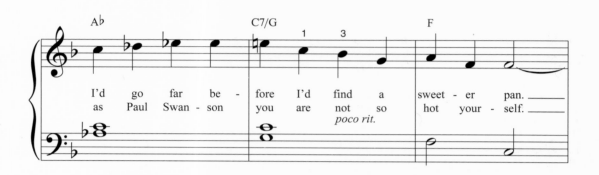

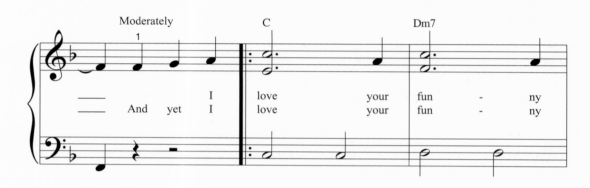

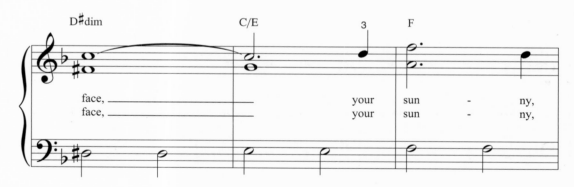

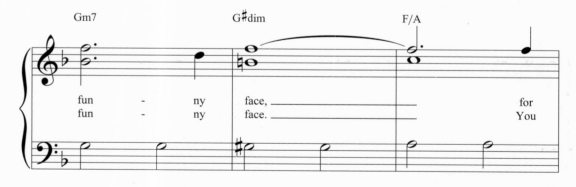

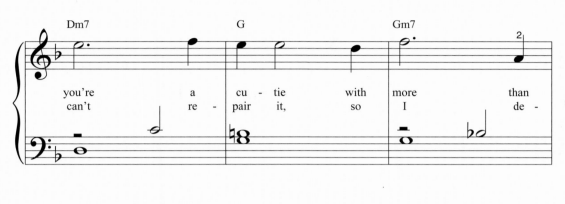

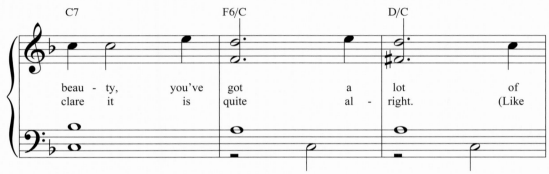

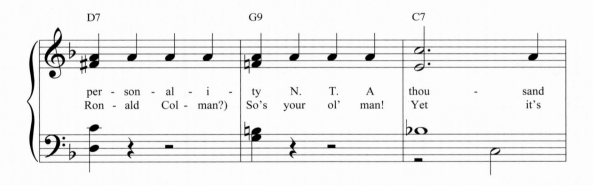

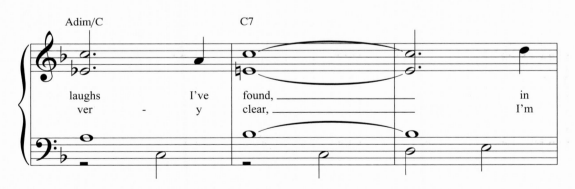

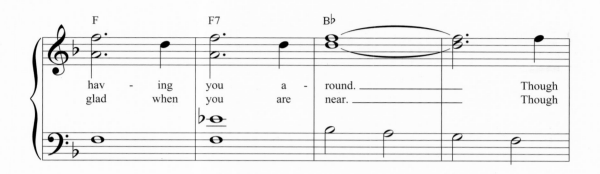

hav - ing you a - round. _____ Though
glad when you are near. _____ Though

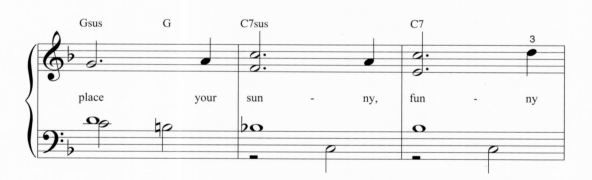

you're no Glo - ria Swan - son,) for worlds I'd not re -
you're no hand - some Har - ry,)

place your sun - ny, fun - ny

face. _____ I   face.

Let's Call the Whole Thing Off

Music and Lyrics by GEORGE GERSHWIN
and IRA GERSHWIN

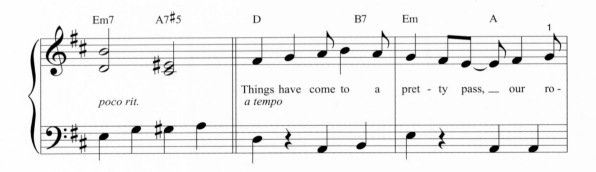

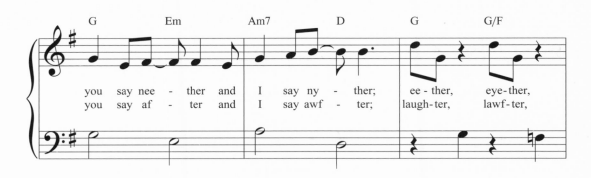

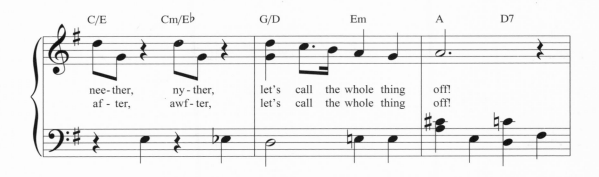

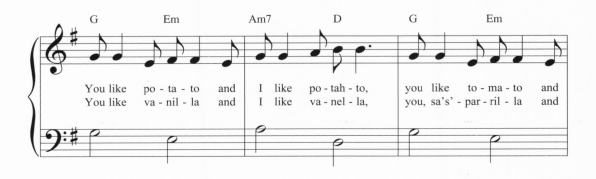

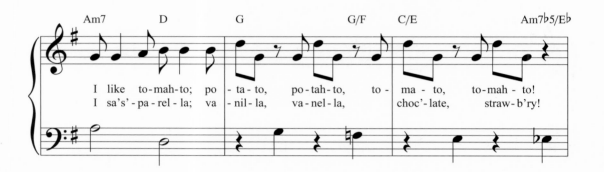

I like to-mah-to; po - ta - to, po-tah-to, to - ma - to, to-mah - to!
I sa's'- pa - rel - la; va -nil - la, va - nel - la, choc'- late, straw-b'ry!

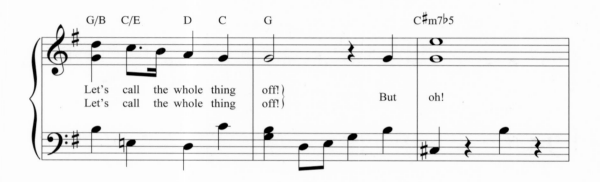

Let's call the whole thing off!⎱
Let's call the whole thing off!⎰   But   oh!

If   we call the whole thing   off,   then   we   must   part.   And

oh!   If   we ev - er part, then   that might break my

Little Jazz Bird

Little Jazz Bird

Music and Lyrics by GEORGE GERSHWIN
and IRA GERSHWIN

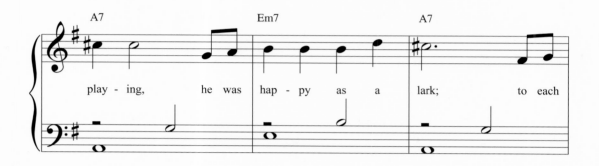

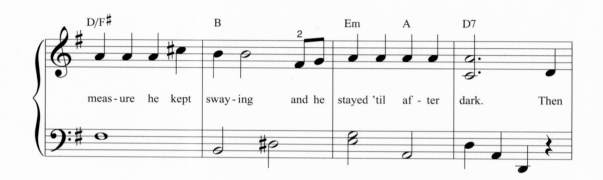

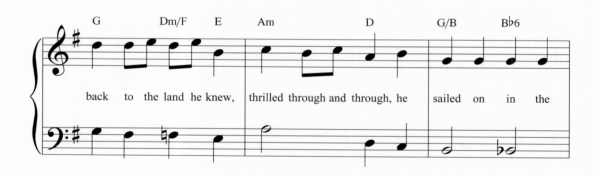

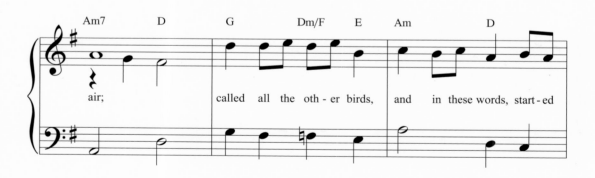

Shall We Dance?

Music and Lyrics by GEORGE GERSHWIN
and IRA GERSHWIN

Brightly, in 2

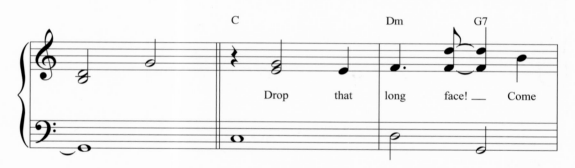

Drop that long face! __ Come

on, have __ a fling! Why keep

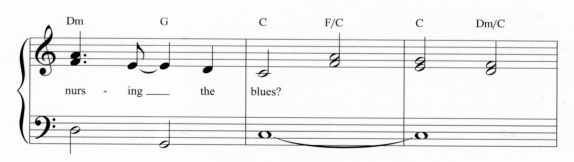

nurs - ing __ the blues?

If   you   want   this ___   old   world   on ___   a

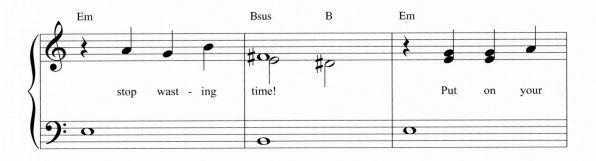

string,   put   on   your   danc - ing   shoes,

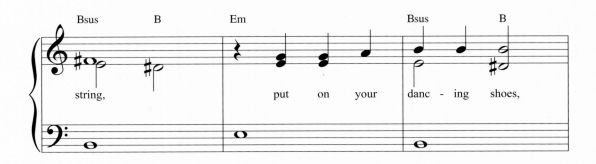

stop   wast - ing   time!   Put   on   your

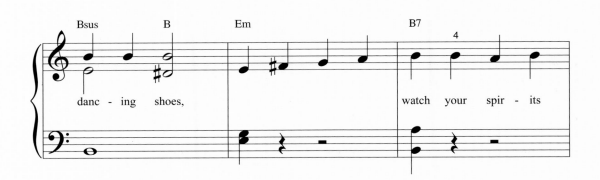

danc - ing   shoes,   watch   your   spir - its

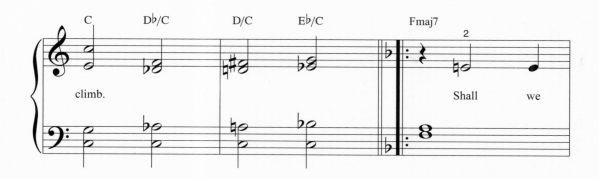

climb.   Shall   we

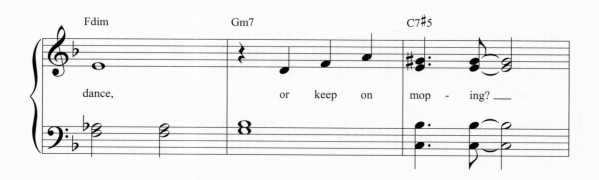

dance,   or   keep   on   mop - ing? ___

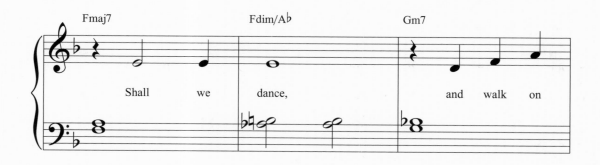

Shall   we   dance,   and   walk   on

air?   Shall   we   give   in ___

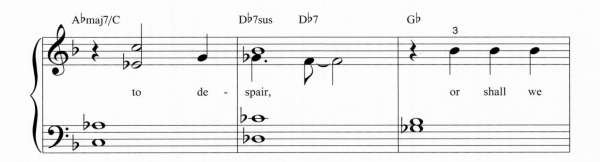

to de - spair,

or shall we

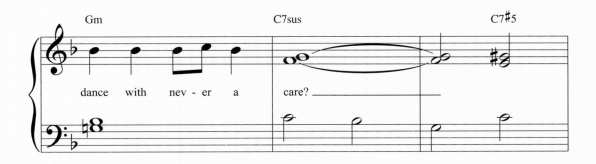

dance with nev - er a care?

Life is short,

we're grow - ing

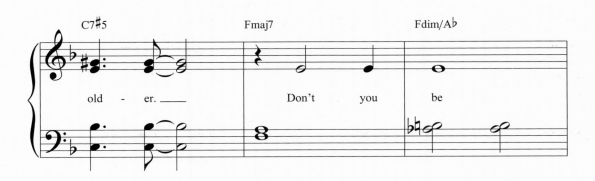

old - er.

Don't you be

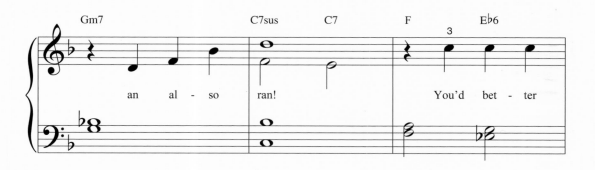

an al - so ran!

You'd bet - ter

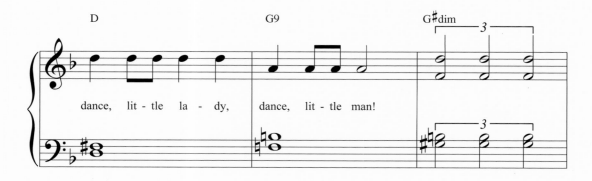

dance, lit - tle la - dy, dance, lit - tle man!

Dance when ev - er you can!

can!

STRIKE UP THE BAND

Music and Lyrics by GEORGE GERSHWIN
and IRA GERSHWIN

Lively March

Let the drums roll out, _____ let the trum-pet call, _____

_____ while the peo-ple shout! _____ Strike up the

band! Hear the cym-bals ring, _____

call - ing   one   and   all _____   to   the

mar - tial   swing! _____   Strike   up   the   band! _____

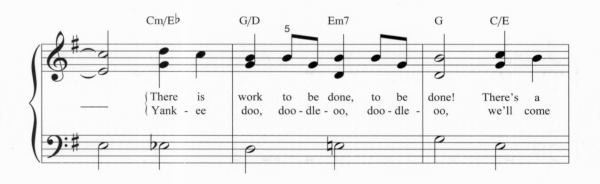

There   is   work   to   be   done,   to   be   done!   There's   a
Yank - ee   doo,   doo - dle - oo,   doo - dle -   oo,   we'll   come

war   to   be   won,   to   be   won!   Come,   you   son   of   a   son   of   a
through, doo - dle - oo,   doo - dle -   oo,   for   the   red,   white and blue,   doo - dle -

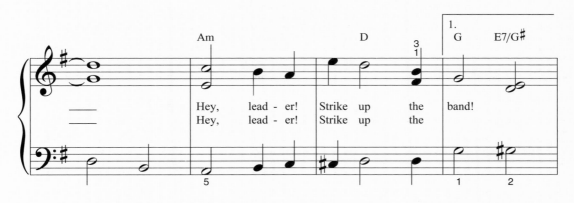

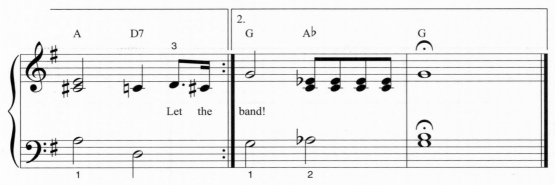

LOVE IS HERE TO STAY

Music and Lyrics by GEORGE GERSHWIN
and IRA GERSHWIN

With motion

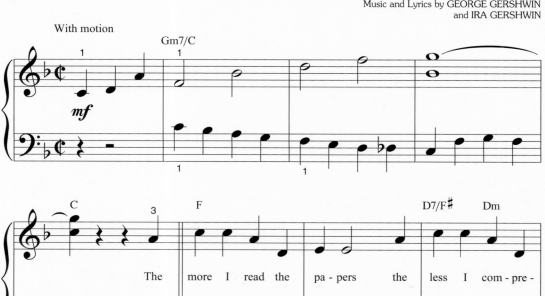

The more I read the pa-pers the less I com-pre-hend the world and all its ca-pers and how it all will end. Noth-ing seems to be last-ing, but

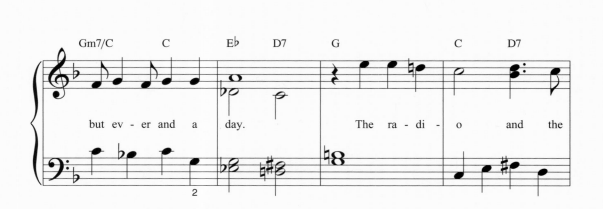

but ev - er and a day. The ra - di - o and the

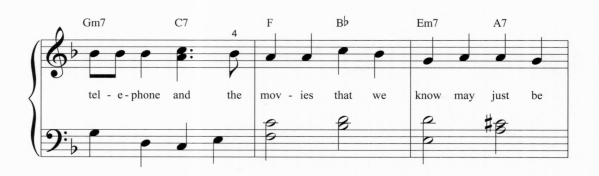

tel - e - phone and the mov - ies that we know may just be

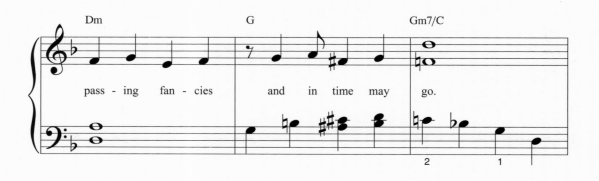

pass - ing fan - cies and in time may go.

But, oh my dear, our love is here to stay;

MY ONE AND ONLY

MY ONE AND ONLY

Music and Lyrics by GEORGE GERSHWIN
and IRA GERSHWIN

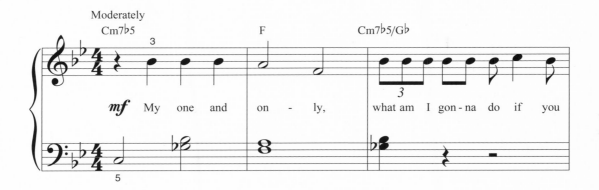

lone - ly, where am I gon-na go if you turn me down? _

Why black - en all my skies of blue? ___

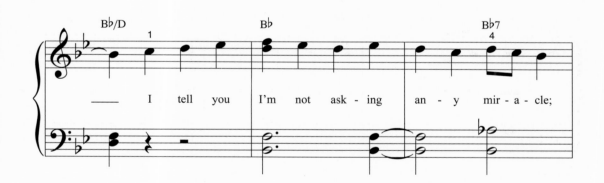

___ I tell you I'm not ask - ing an - y mir - a - cle;

it can be done! It can be done! I know a cler - gy - man who

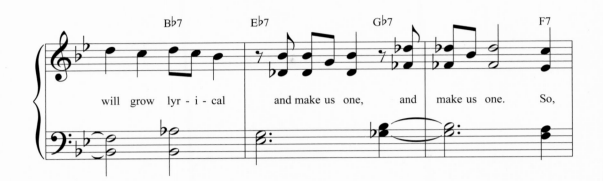

will grow lyr - i - cal   and make us one,   and   make us one.   So,

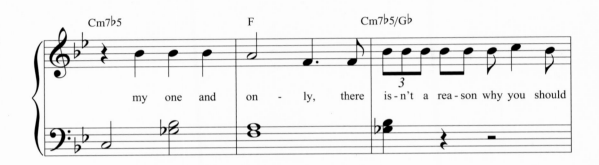

my one and   on - ly,   there   is - n't a rea - son why you should

turn   me   down, __   when I'm so   cra - zy   o - ver

you! _____   you! _____

THE MAN I LOVE

Music and Lyrics by GEORGE GERSHWIN
and IRA GERSHWIN

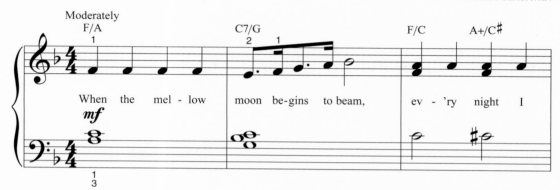

Moderately

When the mel - low moon be-gins to beam, ev - 'ry night I

dream a lit - tle dream, and, of course, Prince Charm-ing is the theme, the

he for me. Al - though I re - al -

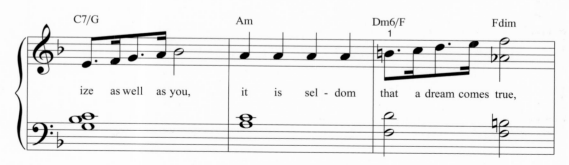

ize as well as you, it is sel - dom that a dream comes true,

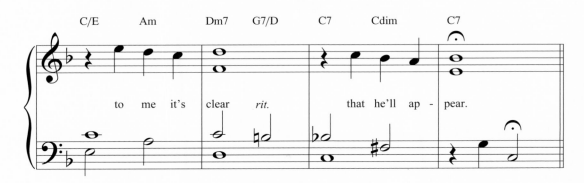

to me it's clear *rit.* that he'll ap - pear.

Moderately slow

F   Fm7/A♭

Some - day he'll come a - long,   the man I love;

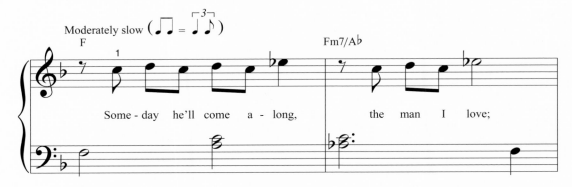

Cm/E♭   D7   Gm7♭5/D♭

and he'll be big and strong,   the man I love;   and when he comes my way,

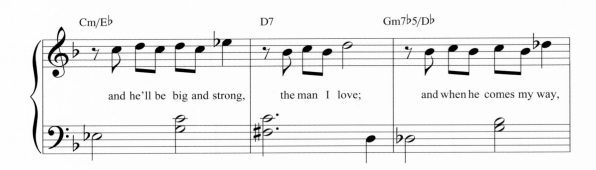

C7   F   Dm7   B♭maj7   C6

I'll do my best to   make   him   stay.

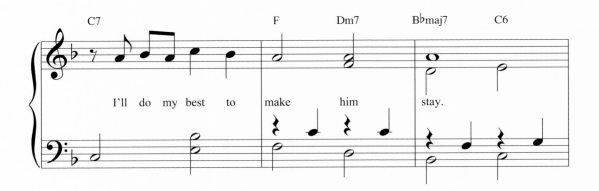

He'll look at me and smile, I'll un-der-stand; and in a lit-tle while

he'll take my hand; and though it seems ab-surd, I know we both won't

say a word. May-be I shall meet him

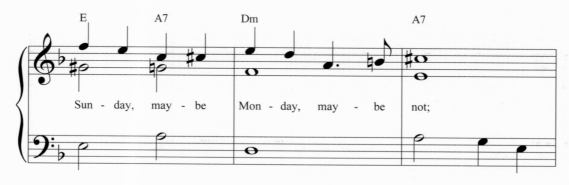

Sun - day, may-be Mon - day, may - be not;

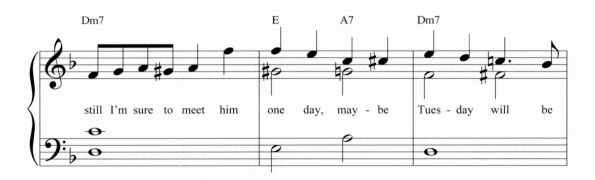

Dm7   E   A7   Dm7

still I'm sure to meet him   one day, may-be   Tues-day will be

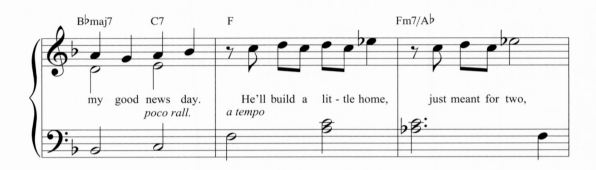

B♭maj7   C7   F   Fm7/A♭

my good news day.   He'll build a lit-tle home,   just meant for two,

poco rall.   *a tempo*

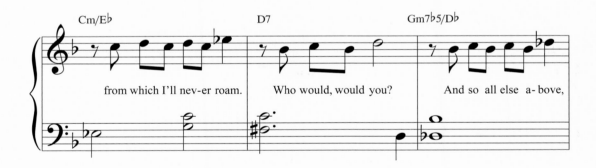

Cm/E♭   D7   Gm7♭5/D♭

from which I'll nev-er roam.   Who would, would you?   And so all else a-bove,

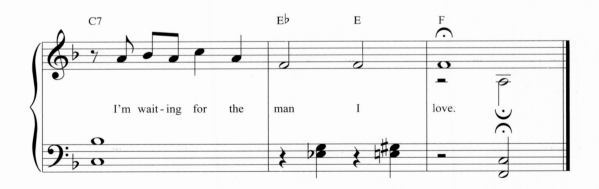

C7   E♭   E   F

I'm wait-ing for the   man   I   love.

NICE WORK IF YOU CAN GET IT

Music and Lyrics by GEORGE GERSHWIN
and IRA GERSHWIN

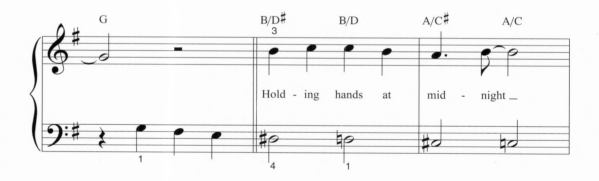

Hold - ing hands at mid - night __

'neath a star - ry sky, nice work __ if you can

get it,   and you can | get it   if   you try.

Stroll - ing   with   the | one   girl _____ | sigh - ing   sigh   af - ter

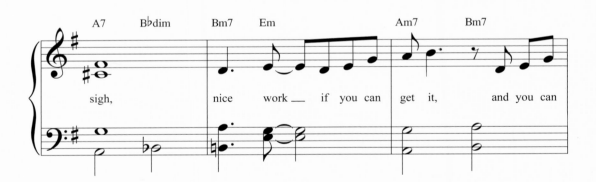

sigh,   nice   work ___ if you can | get   it,   and you can

get   it   if   you   try. _____ | Just   i - mag - ine

nice   work   if you can   get it,   nice   work   if you can

get   it,   nice   work   if you can   get it,   and you can

get   it.   Won't   you   tell   me   how?

Won't   you   tell   me   how?

OF THEE I SING

Music and Lyrics by GEORGE GERSHWIN
and IRA GERSHWIN

lin - ing, you're my sky of blue;

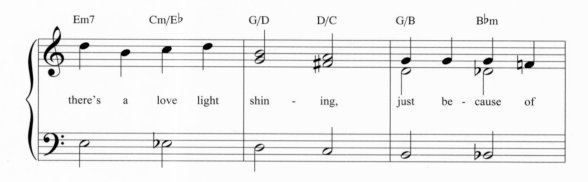

there's a love light shin - ing, just be - cause of

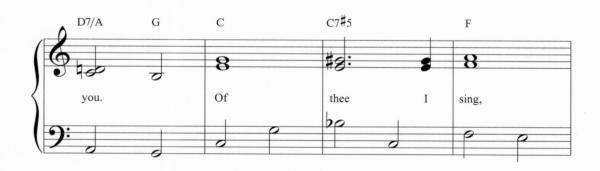

you. Of thee I sing,

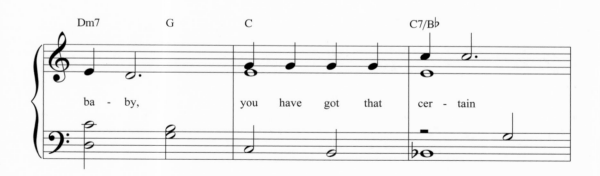

ba - by, you have got that cer - tain

thing,   ba — by!   Shin — ing   star   and

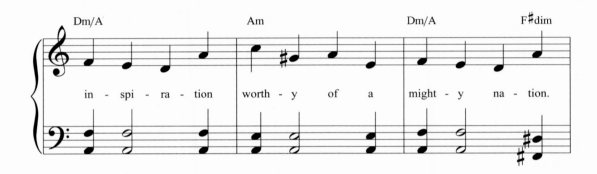

in – spi – ra – tion   worth – y   of   a   might – y   na – tion.

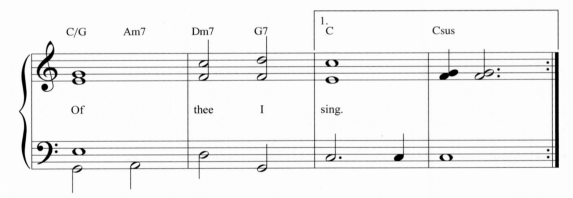

Of   thee   I   sing.

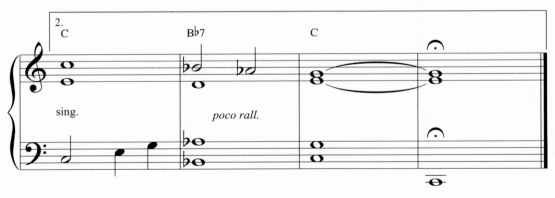

sing.   *poco rall.*

RHAPSODY IN BLUE

By GEORGE GERSHWIN

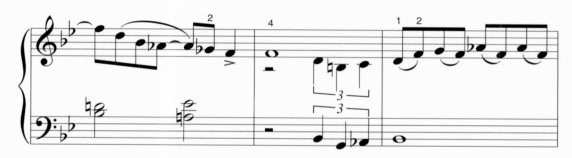

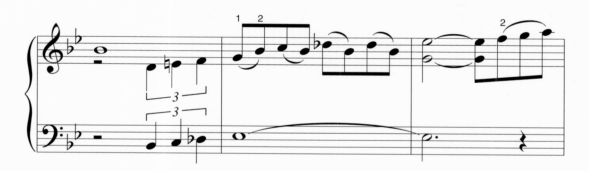

a little faster

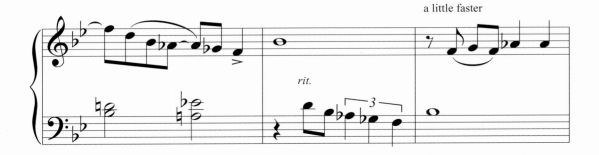

Moderately slow

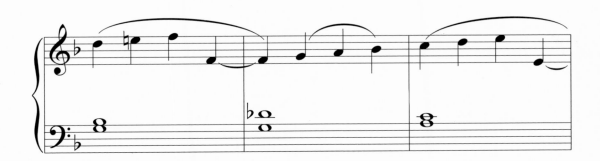

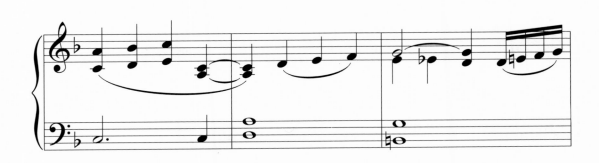

'S Wonderful

Music and Lyrics by GEORGE GERSHWIN
and IRA GERSHWIN

Life has just be - gun.
Don't mind tell - ing you,

Jack has found his Jill.
in my hum - ble fash,

Don't know what you've done,
that you thrill me through

but I'm all a - thrill.
with a ten - der pash.

How can you ex - press
When you said you care,

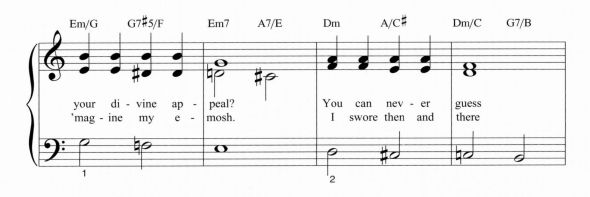

your di - vine ap - peal?
'mag - ine my e - mosh.

You can nev - er guess
I swore then and there

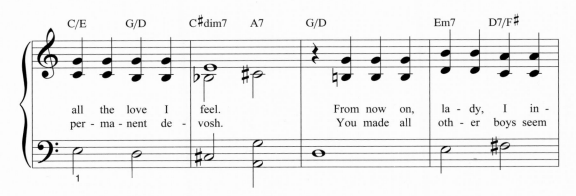

all the love I feel.
per - ma - nent de - vosh.

From now on, lady, I in -
You made all oth - er boys seem

sist
blah.

for me no o - ther girls ex -
Just you a - lone filled me with

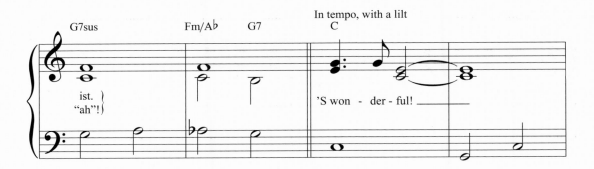

ist.
"ah"!

'S won - der - ful!

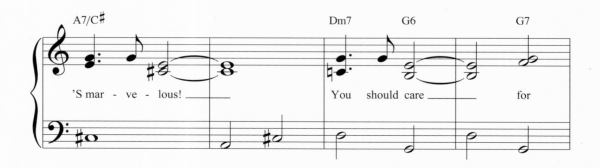

'S mar - ve - lous! _____ You should care _____ for

me! _____ 'S aw - ful nice! _____

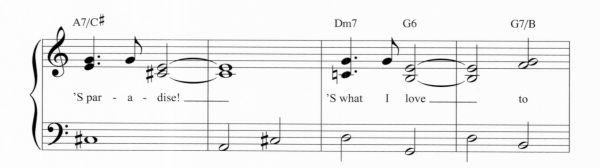

'S par - a - dise! _____ 'S what I love _____ to

see! _____ { You've made { my life so
{ My dear, { it's four - leaf

glam - o - rous.
clo - ver time.

You can't blame me for feel - ing
From now on my heart's work - ing

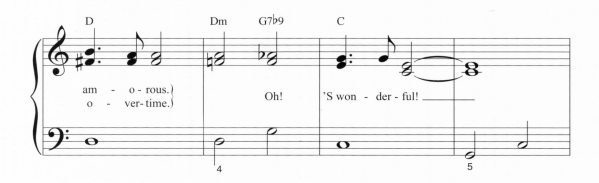

am - o - rous.)
o - ver-time.)

Oh! 'S won - der - ful! ____

'S mar - ve - lous! ____

That you should care for

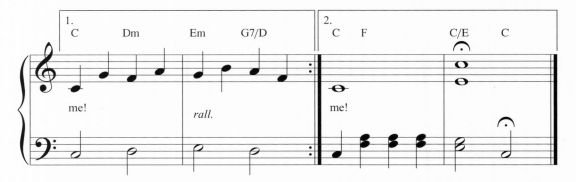

me!

rall.

me!

Someone to Watch Over Me

Someone to Watch Over Me

Music and Lyrics by GEORGE GERSHWIN
and IRA GERSHWIN

found him yet; he's the big af-fair I can-not for-get,

on - ly man I ev - er think of with re - gret.

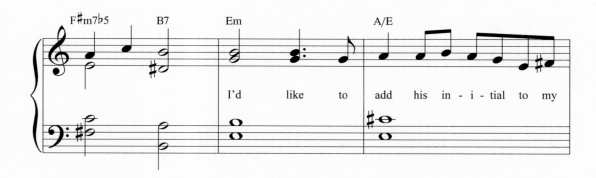

I'd like to add his in - i - tial to my

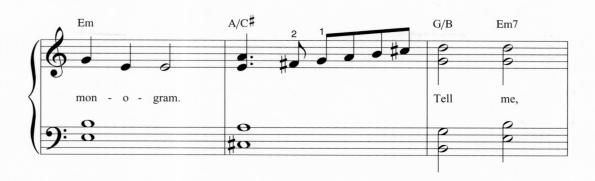

mon - o - gram. Tell me,

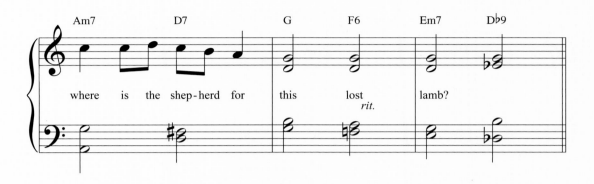

where is the shep-herd for this lost lamb?

rit.

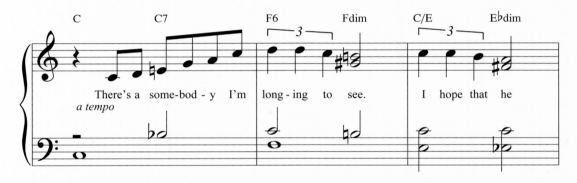

There's a some-bod - y I'm long - ing to see. I hope that he

a tempo

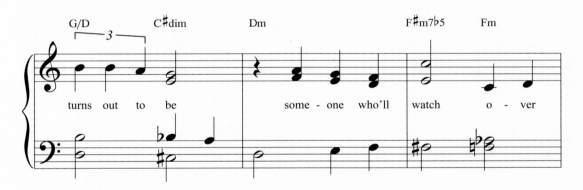

turns out to be some - one who'll watch o - ver

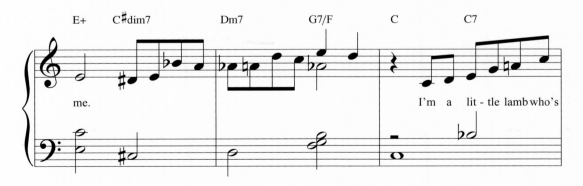

me. I'm a lit - tle lamb who's

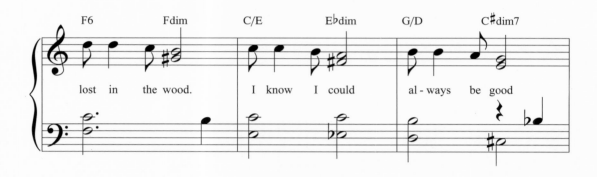

lost in the wood. I know I could al - ways be good

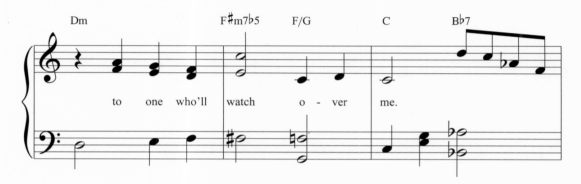

to one who'll watch o - ver me.

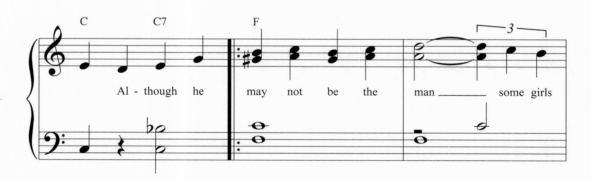

Al - though he may not be the man _____ some girls

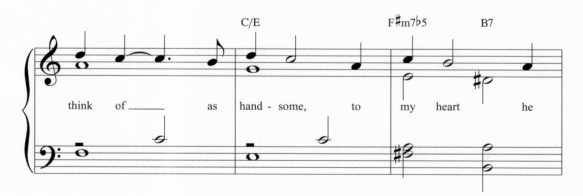

think of _____ as hand - some, to my heart he

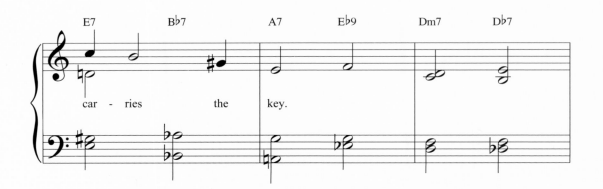

car - ries the key.

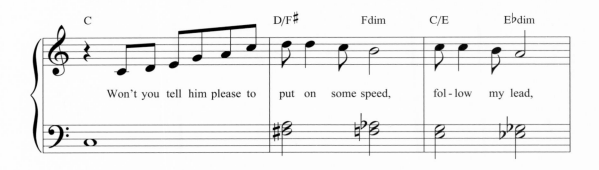

Won't you tell him please to put on some speed, fol - low my lead,

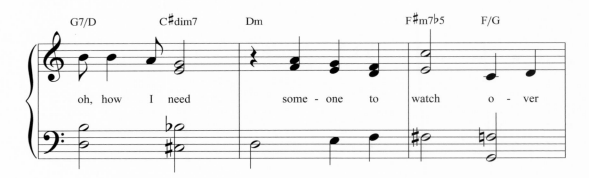

oh, how I need some - one to watch o - ver

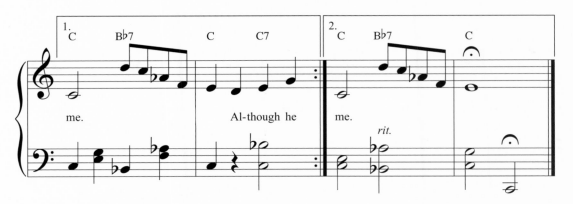

me. Al-though he me.

rit.

THEY ALL LAUGHED

Music and Lyrics by GEORGE GERSHWIN
and IRA GERSHWIN

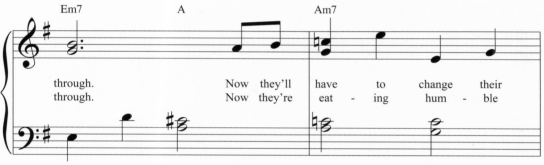

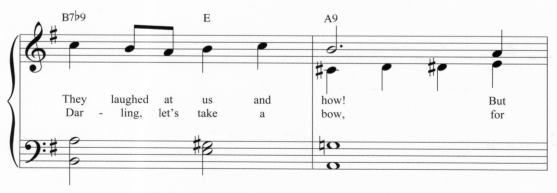

THEY CAN'T TAKE THAT AWAY FROM ME

Music and Lyrics by GEORGE GERSHWIN
and IRA GERSHWIN

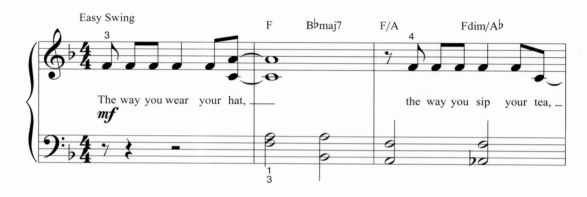

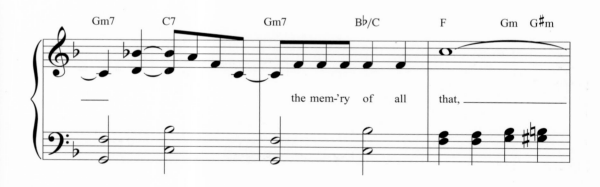

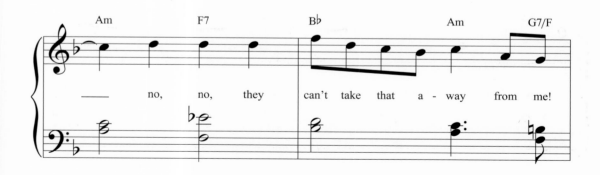